You Can
a Compass

Nevada Public Library

By Lisa Trumbauer

Consultants
David Larwa
National Science Consultant

Nanci R. Vargus, Ed.D.
Assistant Professor of Literacy
University of Indianapolis
Indianapolis, Indiana

Children's Press®
A Division of Scholastic Inc.
New York   Toronto   London   Auckland   Sydney
Mexico City   New Delhi   Hong Kong
Danbury, Connecticut

Designer: Herman Adler Design
Photo Researcher: Caroline Anderson
The photo on the cover shows a girl holding a compass.

Library of Congress Cataloging-in-Publication Data

Trumbauer, Lisa, 1963-
    You can use a compass / by Lisa Trumbauer.
        p. cm. – (Rookie read-about science)
    Includes index.
    Summary: Simple text and photographs describe and illustrate how to use
a compass to find one's way on land, at sea, or in the air.
    ISBN 0-516-22870-6 (lib. bdg.)   0-516-24610-0 (pbk.)
    1. Compass–Juvenile literature. [1. Compass.] I. Title. II. Series.
    QC849.T78 2003
    912'.0284–dc21
                                                        2003000467

CHILDREN'S PRESS, and ROOKIE READ-ABOUT®,
and associated logos are trademarks and or registered trademarks
of Scholastic Library Publishing. SCHOLASTIC and associated logos
are trademarks and or registered trademarks of Scholastic Inc.
1 2 3 4 5 6 7 8 9 10 R 12 11 10 09 08 07 06 05 04 03

How does this hiker
know which way to go?

She has a compass
(KUHM-puhss).

A compass shows
directions. It shows north,
south, east, and west.

A compass looks sort of
like a clock. North is
where the number 12 is
on a clock.

needle

A compass has a needle.
The needle is used to point.
The needle moves to show
which way is north.

The needle moves because it has been magnetized (MAG-nuh-tized). When something is magnetized, it acts like a magnet.

Have you ever used a magnet? Magnets pull some metals toward them.

9

10

A magnet is strongest at each end. The ends are called poles.

A magnet has a north pole and a south pole.

Earth has a magnetic north pole and south pole, too.

The magnetic north pole is in the Arctic.

The magnetic south pole is in Antarctica.

magnetic north pole

magnetic south pole

13

14

Earth's magnetic poles act like the poles on a magnet.

The metal needle of the compass moves. It moves toward Earth's magnetic north or south pole.

How do you use a compass when you are hiking?

You line up the needle with north and south on the compass.

Then north and south are in front of and behind you.

East and west are to the right and left of you.

Hikers also use maps.
A map has a picture of
a compass. It is called
a compass rose.

The compass rose shows
where north, south, east,
and west are on the map.

EXPR...
INTERS...
STATE HI...
MINOR ROA...
HIKING TRAIL
APPALACHIAN TRAIL
RAILROAD
COUNTY BOUNDAR...
TOWNSHIP BOUNDAR...
HIKING REGION BOUNDARY
STATE PARK OR FOREST
WILDERNESS AREA
SCENIC AREA
FORESTED AREA

INTERS...STREAM
...DGE
...TEREST
LOOKOUT TOWER
GATE OR CHAIN
TRAIL SHELTER
TRAIL HUT
RECREATION SITE, CAMPING FACILITIES
RECREATION SITE, DAY USE ONLY
CAMPSITE (TENTSITES)
DISTRICT RANGER STATION

KILOMETERS

MILES

SCALE: 1:100,000   1 centimeter on the map represents 1 kilometer on the ground
Approximately 5/8" equals 1 mile on the ground   CONTOUR INTERVAL

Compasses can look very
different, but they all do
the same thing.

Put ten compasses in a row.
Their needles will all point
in the same direction.

24

Many people use compasses. People use compasses when they need to know which way to go.

Sailors use compasses to help them find their way on the open sea.

How do pilots know
which way to fly when
their airplanes are in
the clouds?

They use a compass.

People use compasses
so they don't get lost.
A compass helps show
which way to go.

Which way should this
hiker go?

Words You Know

airplane

compass

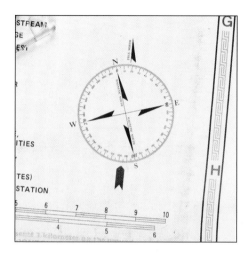

compass rose

magnet

needle

Index

About the Author

As a student, Lisa Trumbauer found science a mystery. Now the author of nearly two hundred books for children, Lisa enjoys unlocking the mystery of science by writing about it in ways that kids—and she—can understand. Lisa lives in New Jersey with one dog, two cats, and her husband, Dave.

Photo Credits